FABULOUS
FASHION

Buster Books

Illustrated by Nellie Ryan
Edited by Elizabeth Scoggins
Designed by Barbara Ward

First published in Great Britain in 2011 by Buster Books,
an imprint of Michael O'Mara Books Limited,
9 Lion Yard, Tremadoc Road,
London SW4 7NQ

W www.busterbooks.co.uk   f Buster Children's Books   🐦 @BusterBooks

A CIP catalogue record for this book is available
from the British Library.

ISBN: 978-1-907151-84-2

4 6 8 10 9 7 5 3

This book was printed in September 2014 by
Bookwell Limited, Teollisuustie 4, FIN-06100, Porvoo, Finland.

Papers used by Michael O'Mara Books are natural, recyclable products made from
wood grown in sustainable forests. The manufacturing processes conform to the
environmental regulations of the country of origin.

FABULOUS FASHION

A gorgeous new magazine

Go behind the scenes of this stylish new fashion magazine. It is full of stunning designs for you to complete and colour any way you please.

Meet the creative team who put *Fabulous Fashion* together. Add your own creative touches and design-inspiration to the outfits featured in the Spring, Summer, Autumn and Winter Issues. You're sure to find inspiration, whatever the weather!

When Fashion Week comes along, you'll get the chance to go wild, taking designs straight from catwalk to oh-so cool – then, get creative with the past with vintage style to die for.

Finally, when the awards season begins, it's time to add a touch of glamour to the Red-Carpet Issue.

So go on – put your stamp on style.

MEET THE TEAM

Meet the editor-in-chief.

This stylish lady has
the final word on elegance.

Complete her office
space with the ultimate
in designer style.

The Style Team.

Fashion
photographer.

Stylist to the stars.

Journalist about town.

Editor at large.

These ladies in the magazine 'biz' need outfits to shout about.

A wardrobe to die for!

Fill the stylist's shelves and rails with
every outfit you can imagine.

The make-up artist at work.

Complete her make-up look.

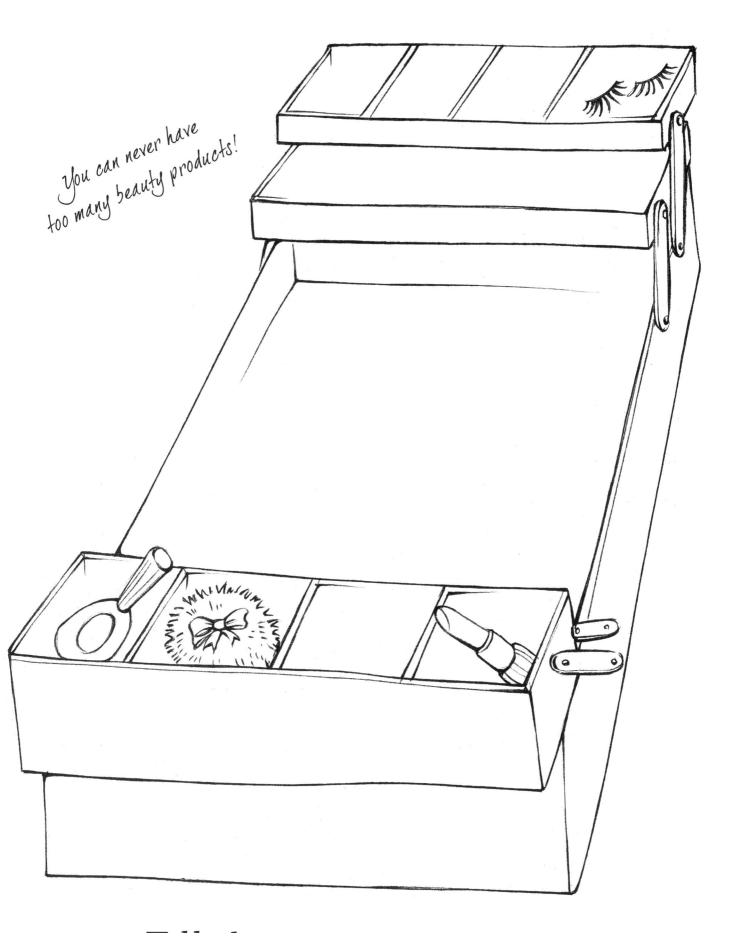

You can never have too many beauty products!

Fill the vanity case.

Choosing models for the first issue.

Work it!

Wow!

Spring

Winter

What did they wear to the casting?

Own it!

So now!

Fall

Summer

More amazing models ...

Who would you
pick to be
cover girl?

Give them outfits fit
for a fashion shoot.

Cover girl!

Create a cool
cover-girl haircut
for the first issue.

THE SPRING ISSUE

Boutique bliss.

Complete the window displays with perfect designs for a Parisian shopper's paradise.

What a haul!

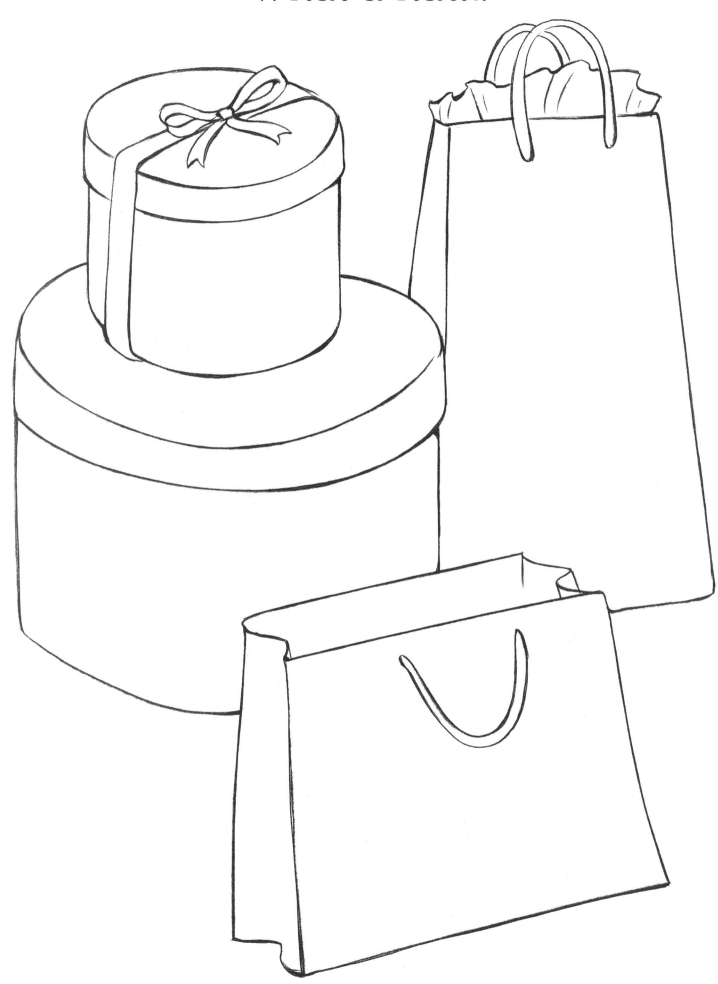

Decorate the bags and
boxes from your
favourite boutiques.

Shopping with style.

Dress these ladies to impress as they shop 'til they drop.

A Valentine's match!

Give this couple matching outfits for a romantic evening.

He loves me – he loves me not.

Add bright florals and pretty pastels and surround her with spring blossoms.

Meadow heaven.

Sprinkle their outfits with glorious garlands of flowers.

FASHION FOCUS:
Spring Fling
Add the finishing touches to these stylish dresses.

Girls just love to dance!

FASHION FOCUS:
Fierce Fashion!

Jazz up these jumpsuits
with funky tribal patterns.

It's all the rage.

Design your own tribal print,
then decorate her outfit with it.

Spring prints
are so
charming.

Design your own swatches
of pretty prints for spring.

From daytime perfection ...

Give these daytime outfits
finishing touches to make
them evening-wear ready
in a trice.

Accessories are everything!

... to evening
sensation.

Co-ordination is key.

Decorate these items to make them go together and give your outfit the match factor.

A real bangle of joy.

Feathers and trims for a fine fascinator.

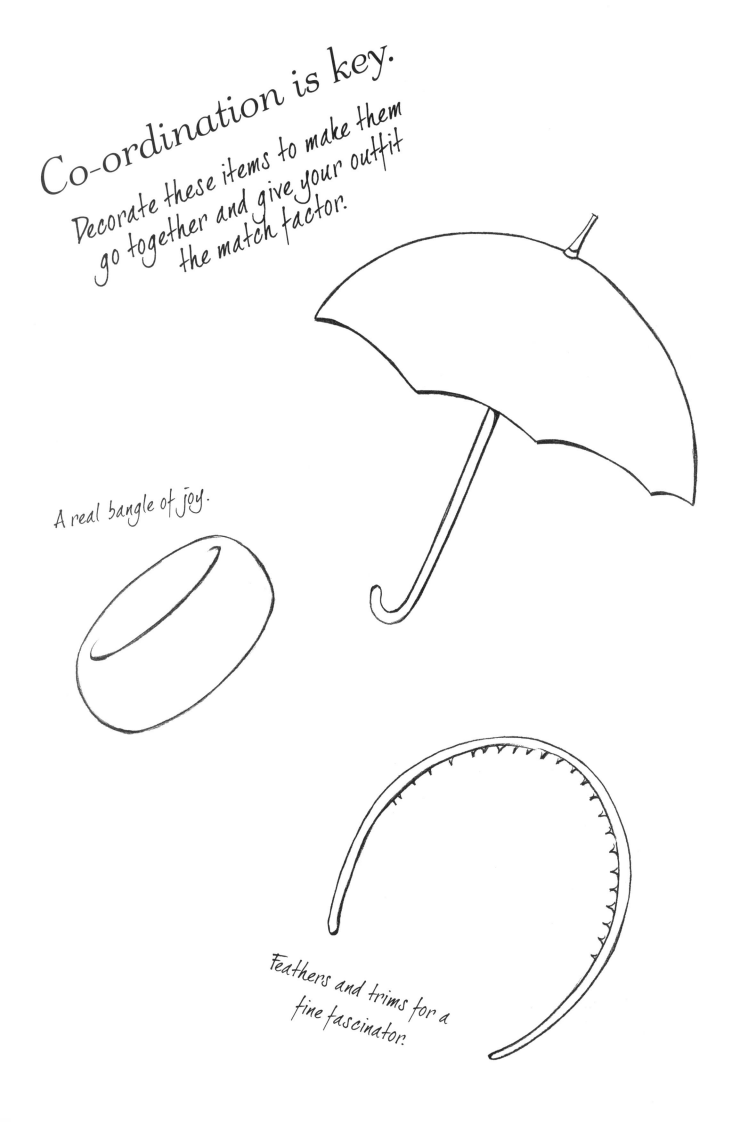

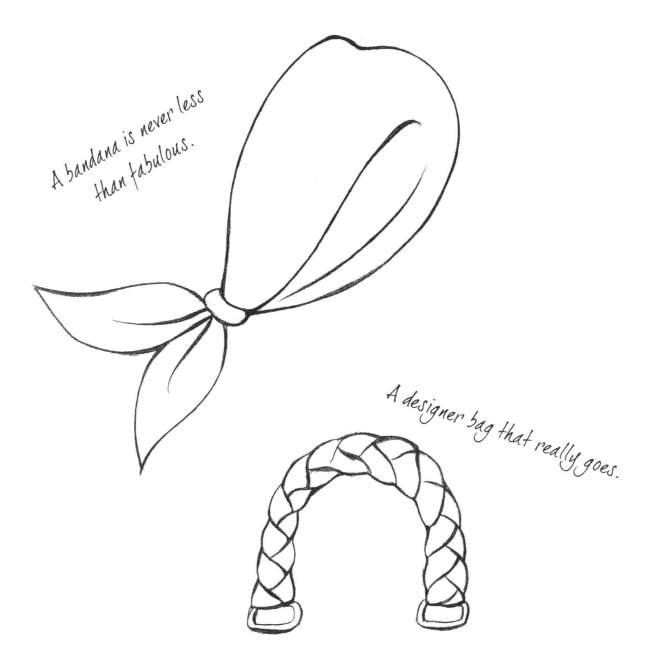

A bandana is never less than fabulous.

A designer bag that really goes.

There's no rain on this fashion parade!

Sprinkle the Wellington boots and
raincoats with stylish designs.

This season's essential 'It' bag.

Design a must-have handbag for chic spring evenings.

THE SUMMER ISSUE

FASHION FOCUS:
Anchors Away!

Add large collars, stripes, and rope-and-anchor details to these designs.

Nautical never goes out of style.

FASHION FOCUS:
Lace Luxury

Finish off these dresses with stylish lace and pretty broderie anglaise.

Fresh lace makes for feminine frocks.

Create a pretty, lacy pattern of your own.

Picnic perfection.

Complete their outfits for outdoor success.

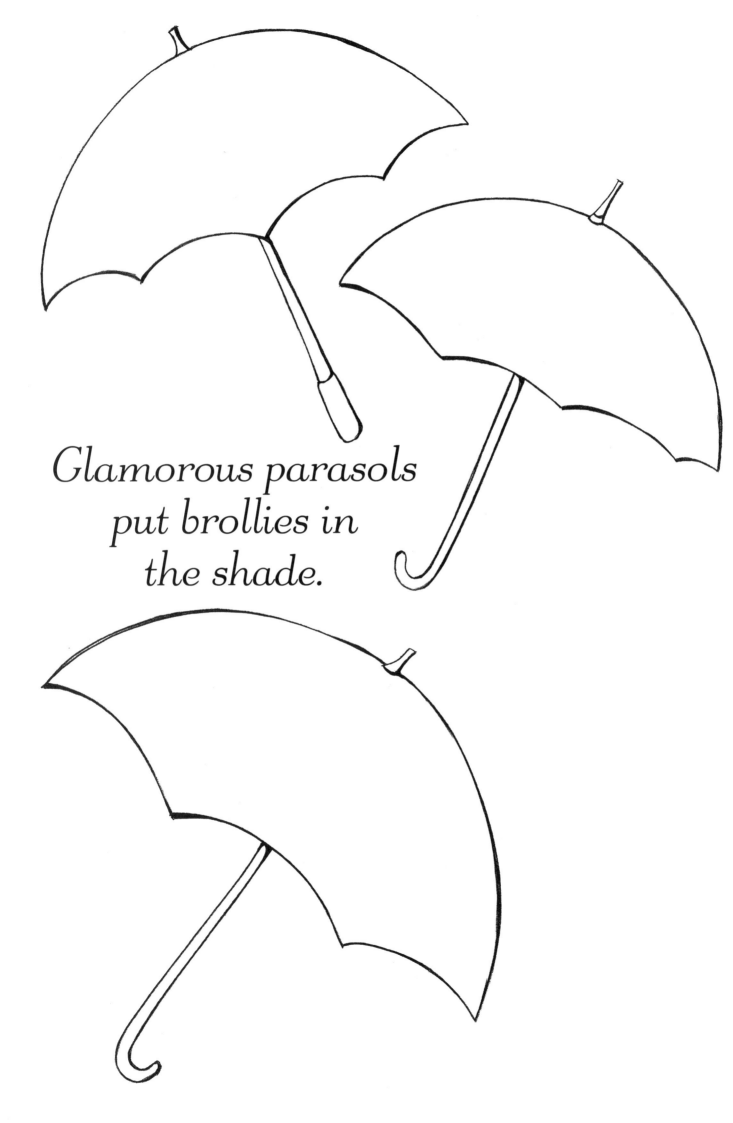

Glamorous parasols put brollies in the shade.

Add ruffles and bows for a perfect day in the sun.

Get the sunbathing factor.

Add pattern perfection to these sunny girls' swimsuits.

Decorate their towels, too.

Surf's up, ladies!

Ride a wave of inspiration to design brilliant board shorts, wetsuits and surfboards.

Get ruffled!

Add ribbons and bows,
and pleats and frills
for a seasonal flounce.

A summer ball ...

... *means gorgeous gowns.*

Complete these glamorous outfits with black-tie style - perfect for dancing the night away.

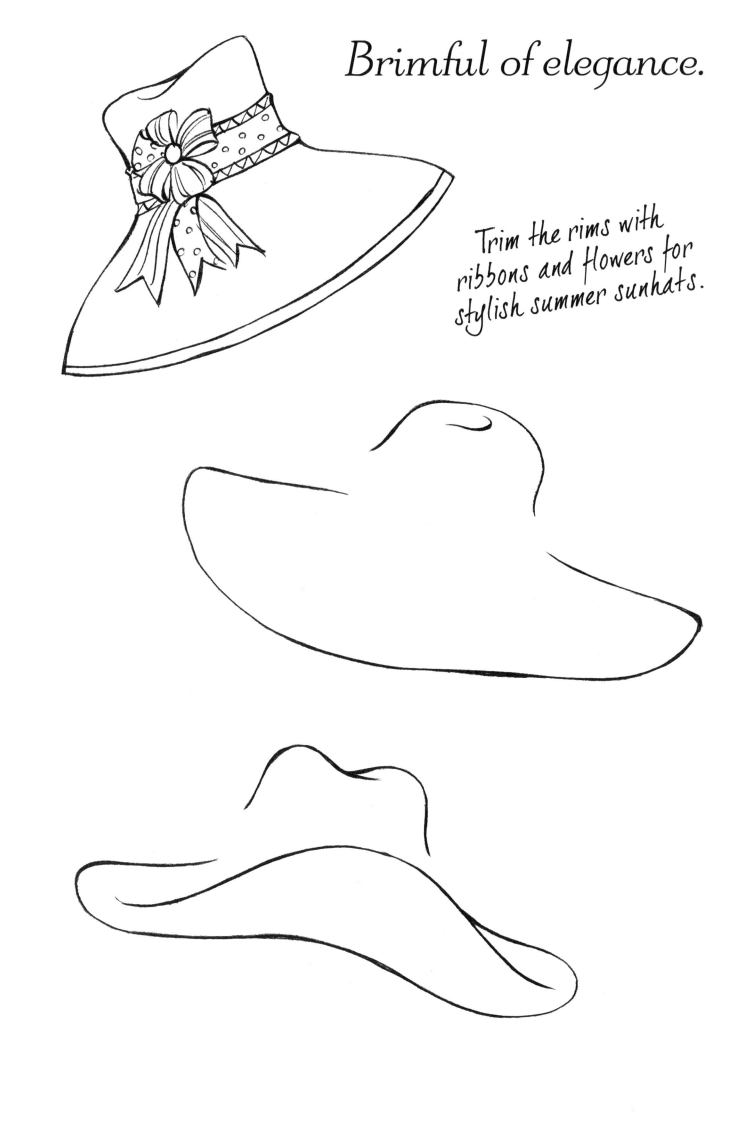

Brimful of elegance.

Trim the rims with ribbons and flowers for stylish summer sunhats.

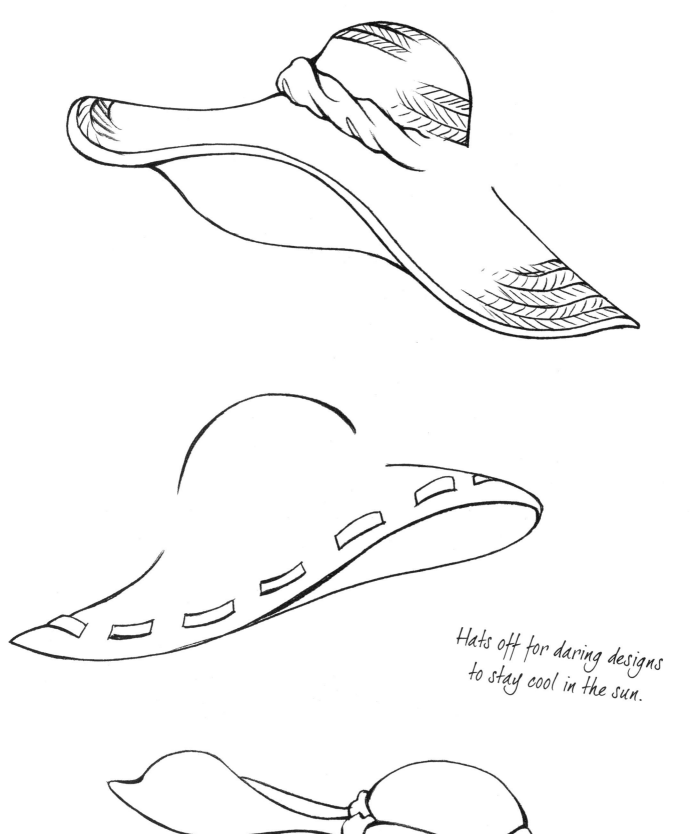

Hats off for daring designs
to stay cool in the sun.

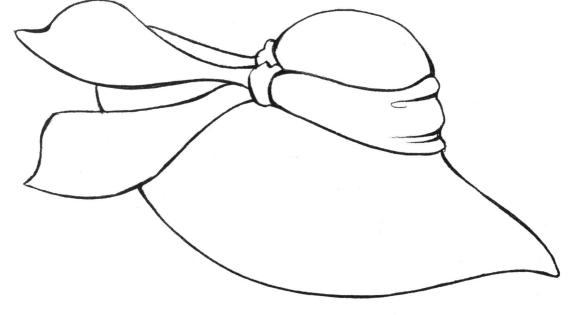

Fabulous fabrics.

Cover her picnic blanket in a patchwork of pattern.

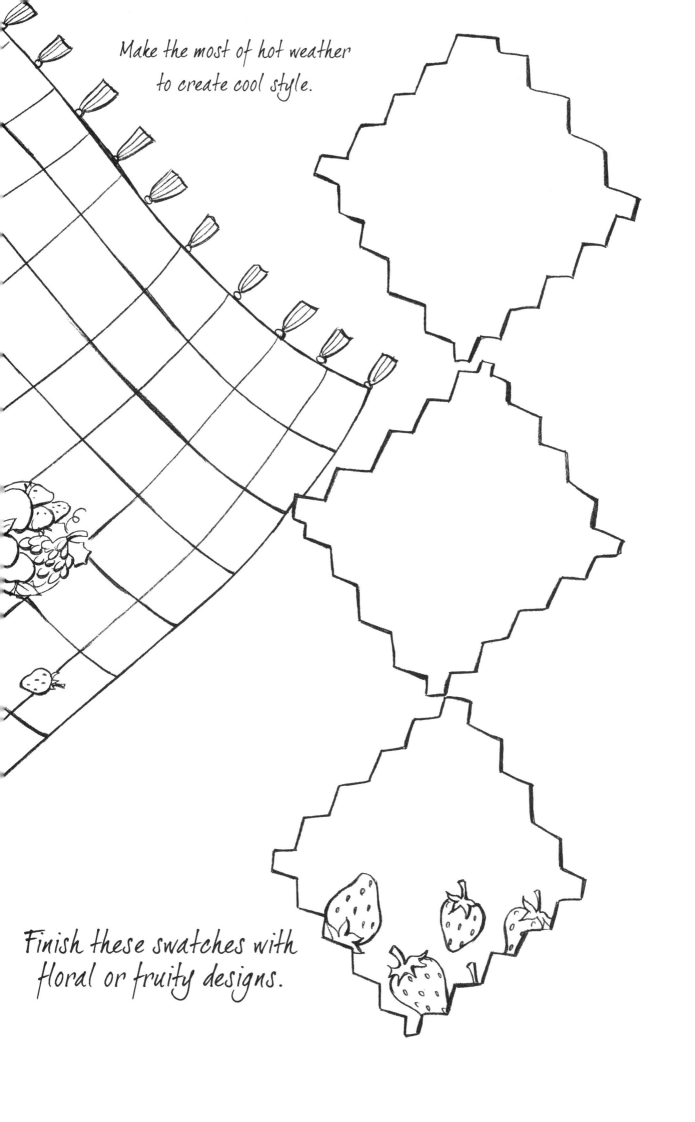

Make the most of hot weather
to create cool style.

Finish these swatches with
floral or fruity designs.

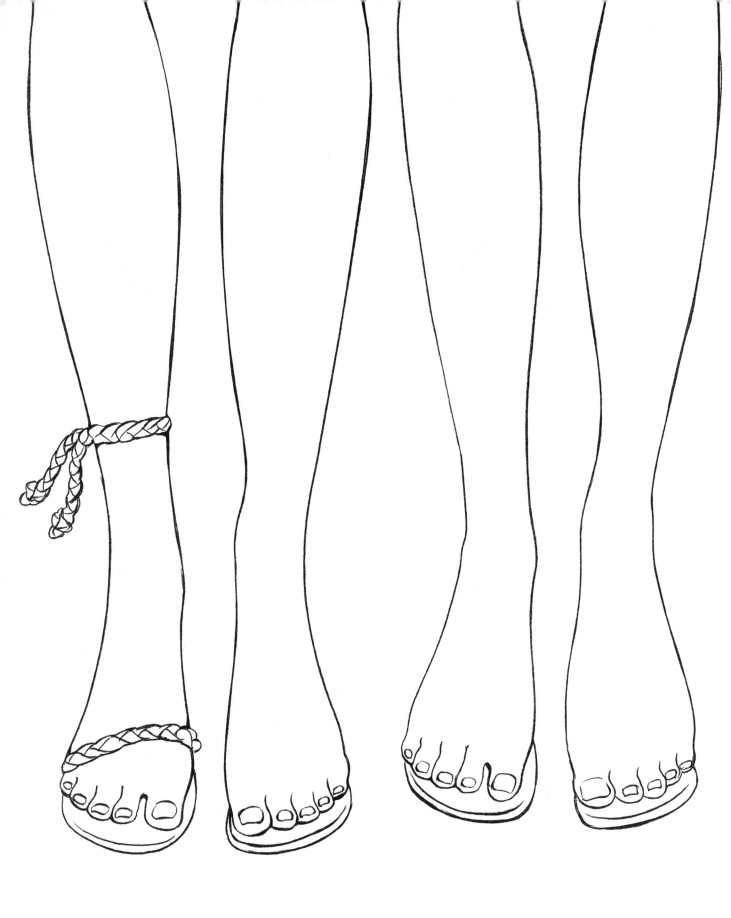

Footloose and fancy-free!

Give the models sassy summer pedicures
and stylish sandals.

THE FASHION-WEEK

ISSUE

Front-row fashionistas.

What are these fashion-forward ladies wearing?

Ahead of the rest with hats to die for.

Add feathers, bows, buttons
and jewels to make these hats
the envy of everyone!

A sprinkling of stardust style!

Turn up the volume with super shoulder pads and glam-rock glitz.

Made for mystery.

Add feathers and frills to
magnificent masks and glorious gowns
for a historical ball.

Cream of the catwalk.

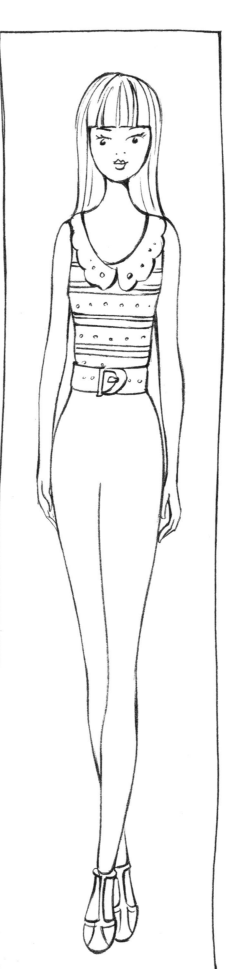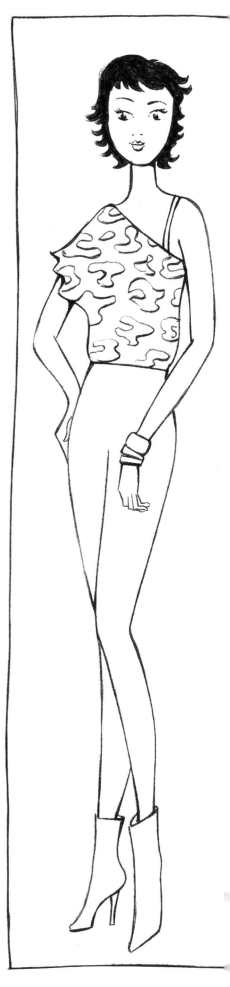

Complete the editor's favourite Fashion-Week outfits.

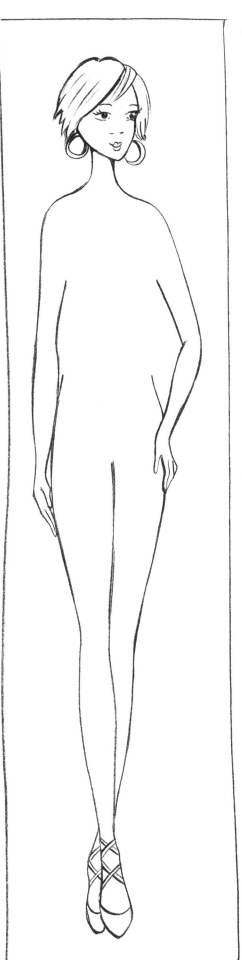
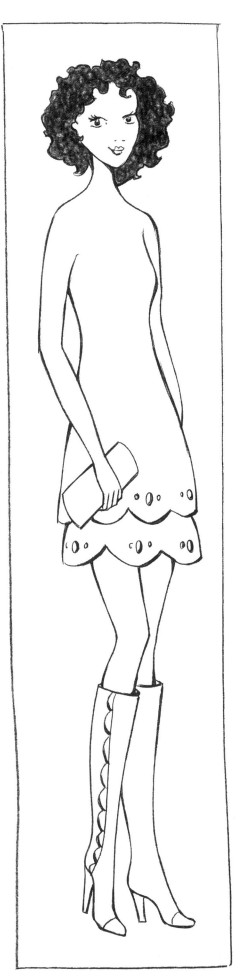

Dance spectacular.

Design a dazzling ballerina-inspired dress for the fashion-show finale.

Dance-floor diva.

Everyone's anticipating the amazing after-show party, but what should the DJ wear?

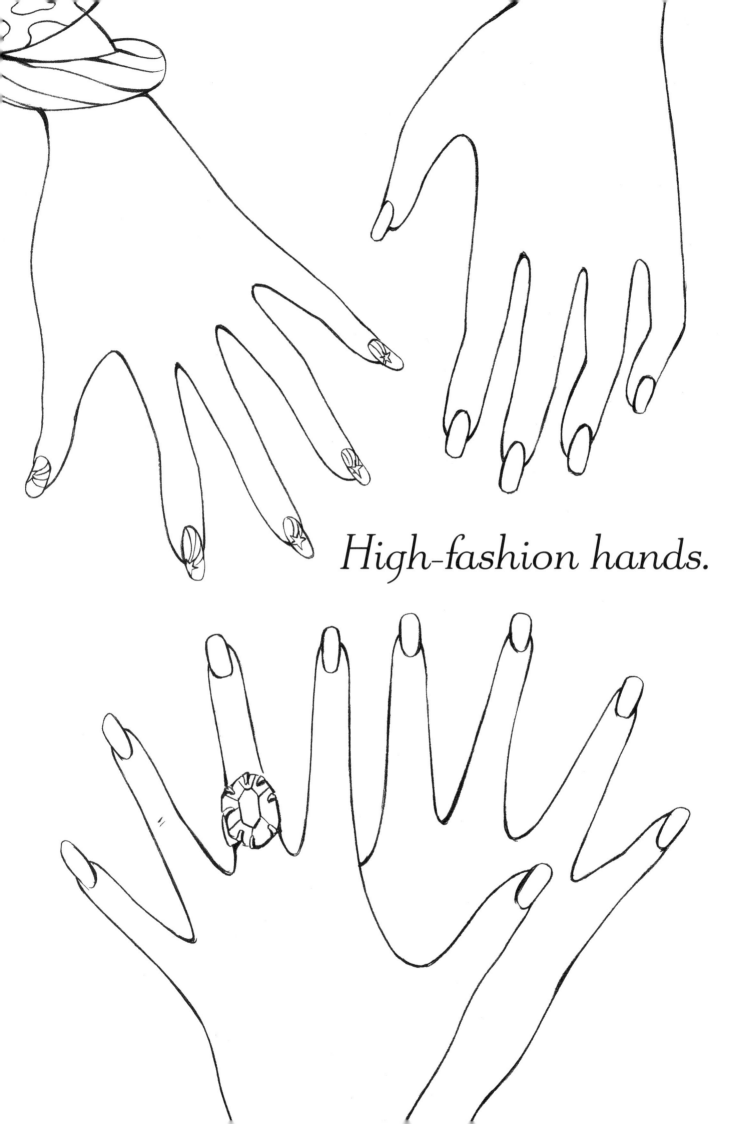

High-fashion hands.

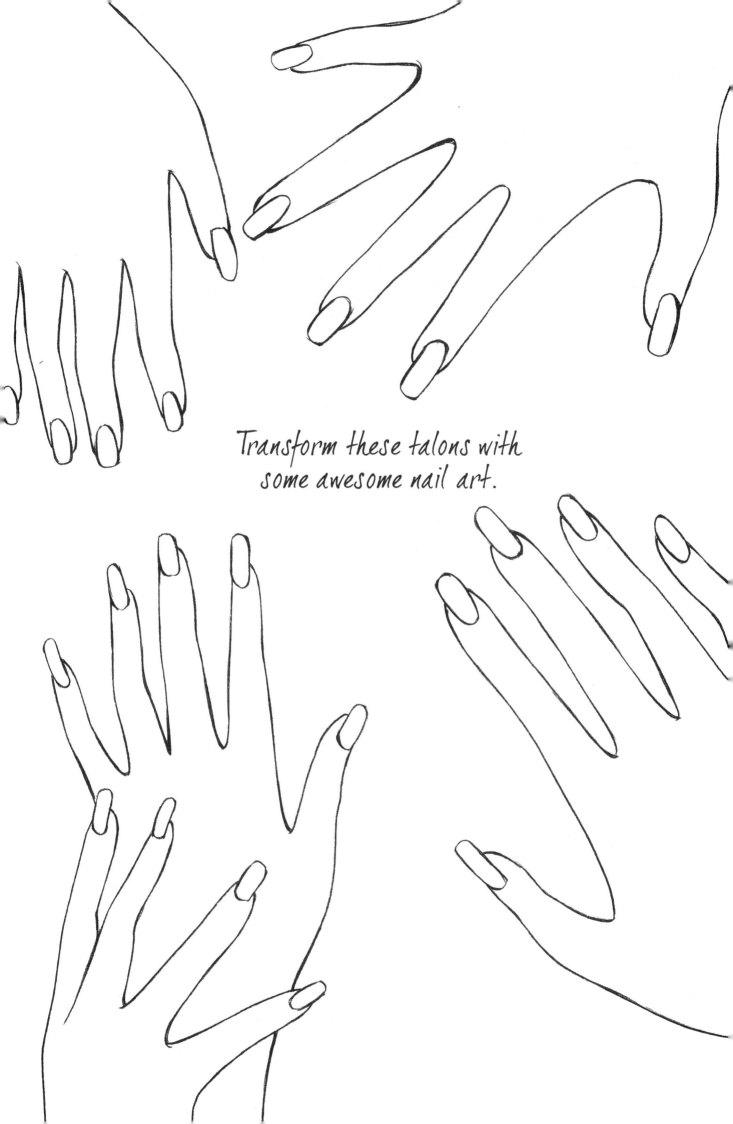

Transform these talons with
some awesome nail art.

Out of this world!

Add some fantastic finishing touches to these futuristic fashions - be as inventive as you dare.

Face the music.

Give her a make-up look that everyone will be talking about.

THE AUTUMN ISSUE

Animal prints are a roaring success.

Add spots and stripes to these dresses for that extra 'wow' factor.

FASHION FOCUS:
Ready, Preppy, Go!

Finish with neat blazers, stripy knitwear, pleated skirts and tailored trousers.

Perfect preppy outfits are in a class of their own.

FASHION FOCUS:
Steampunk Scene

Get some gothic glamour with
cool Victorian-style dresses
and accessories.

A Transylvanian revamp!

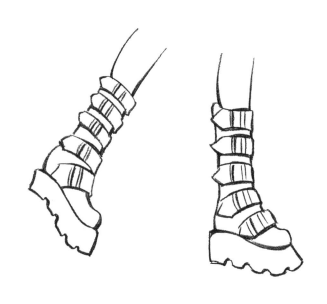

FASHION FOCUS:
Charge of the
Chic Brigade

Add military magic and soldier style to complete these outfits and make them stand to attention.

That's an order!

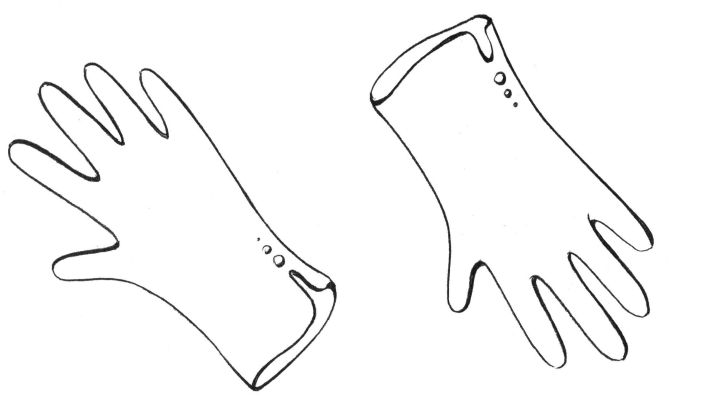

Fingers, thumbs and woolly mitts.

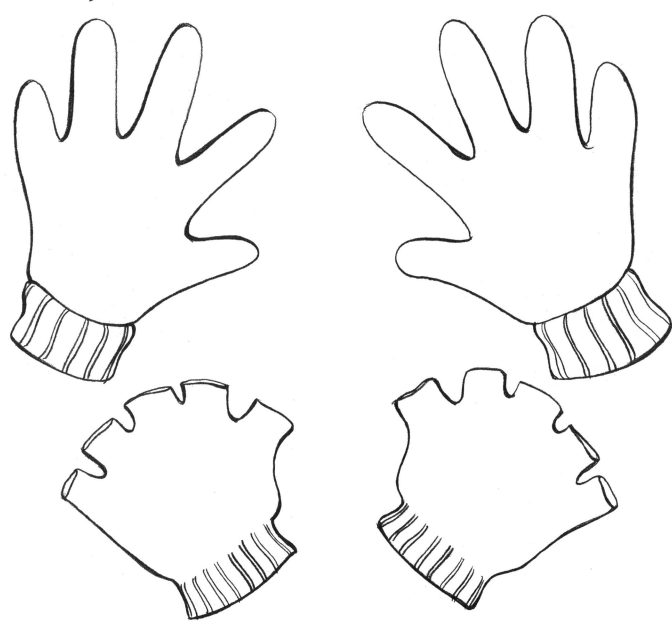

Make these gloves lovely with fabulous finishing touches.

Sleepover style-out.

Create some pretty prints
and sassy patterns for
these nightwear sets.

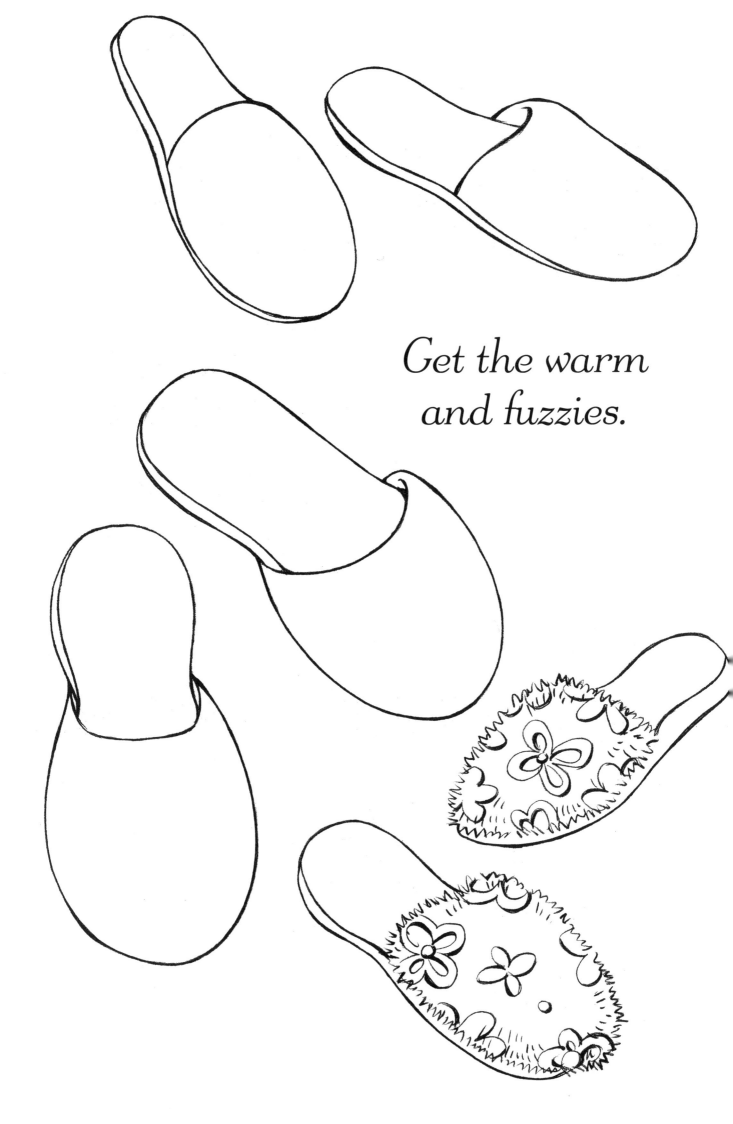

Get the warm
and fuzzies.

Slip into something cosy – add cute designs for fashionable feet to relax in.

Park life!

Design doggie-togs and
outdoor garments and
make each outfit match.

FASHION FOCUS:
So Boho,
So Beautiful

Finish these fantastic
flowing dresses with
far-out patterns.

Beyond fabulous, darling!

Fashion's flying high.

Get these
models ready for
take-off as they
channel the glamour
of aviation's
golden age.

THE VINTAGE ISSUE

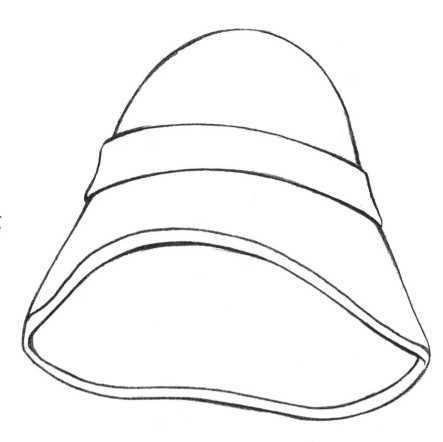

Magnificent
millinery.

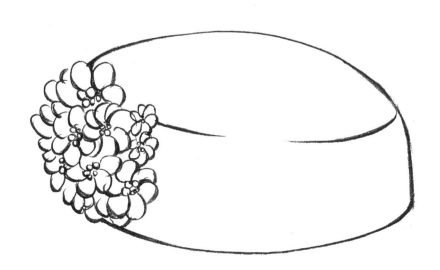

Get the elegance of another era by adding cool decorations to these classic hats.

FASHION FOCUS:
Capability Cool

Add big buttons and bold patterns to these cloche hats and cool capes.

A seal of approval for forties-style elegance.

Shake, rattle
and roll, ladies!

Add the finishing touches to
these prom-dress delights.

FASHION FOCUS:
Mad About Style

A touch of decoration and these sixties-inspired outfits will be perfectly poised to grace the fashion pages.

Oh-so sweet!

Design your own pattern to add to these dresses and really put them in the swing.

A flare affair.

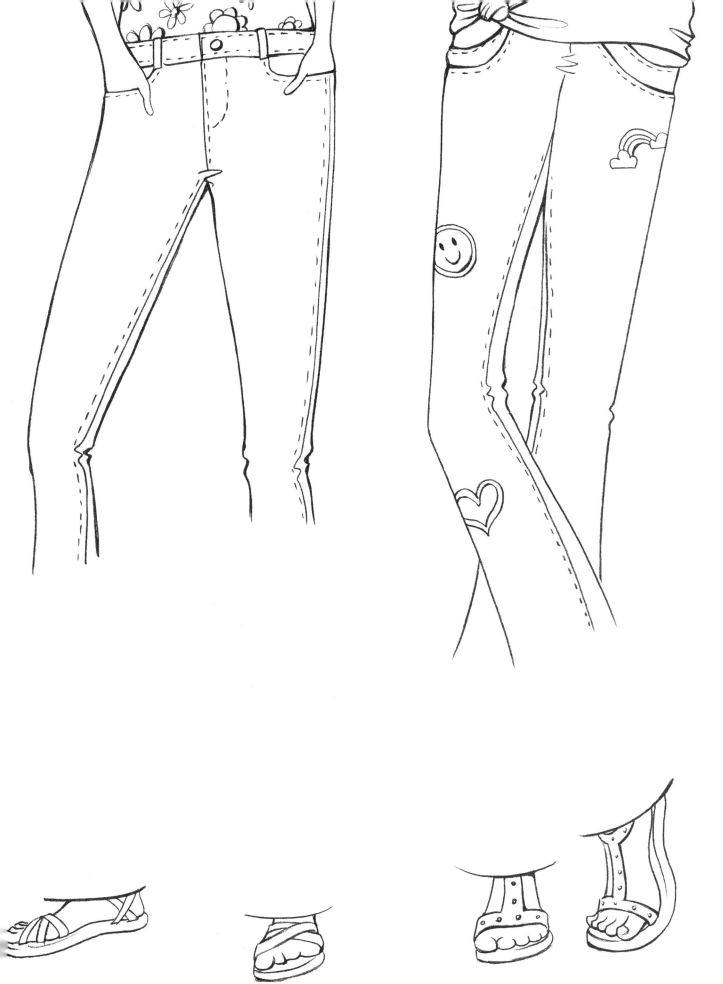

Flare these trousers as wide as you dare
- add funky motifs to finish the look.

FASHION FOCUS:
Maxi-heaven

Pretty patchwork and paisley patterns bring out the power in these seventies flowers.

Right on!

FASHION FOCUS:
Punk Perfect

These models need more rips, tears, badges and bite.

Never mind the posh frocks – here come the punks!

Awesome eighties.

Add neon brights and bold geometric prints.

THE WINTER ISSUE

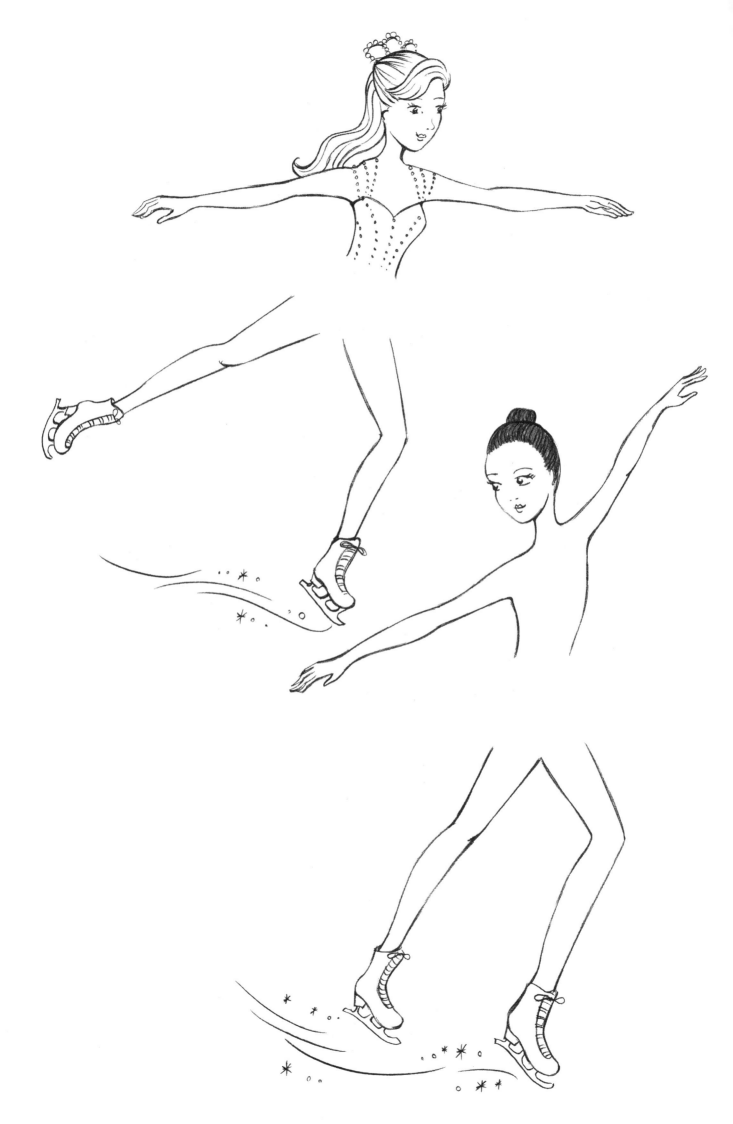

Skate sweethearts.

Add ruffles, pleats and
sequin designs to make
these girls cut an
impressive figure on the ice.

Get knitted this winter.

Add designs to these
over-sized jumpers and
toasty leg-warmers for
chilly winter days and
cosy nights at home.

Skate sensation.

Decorate the skating boots
and make them perfect for
an ice princess.

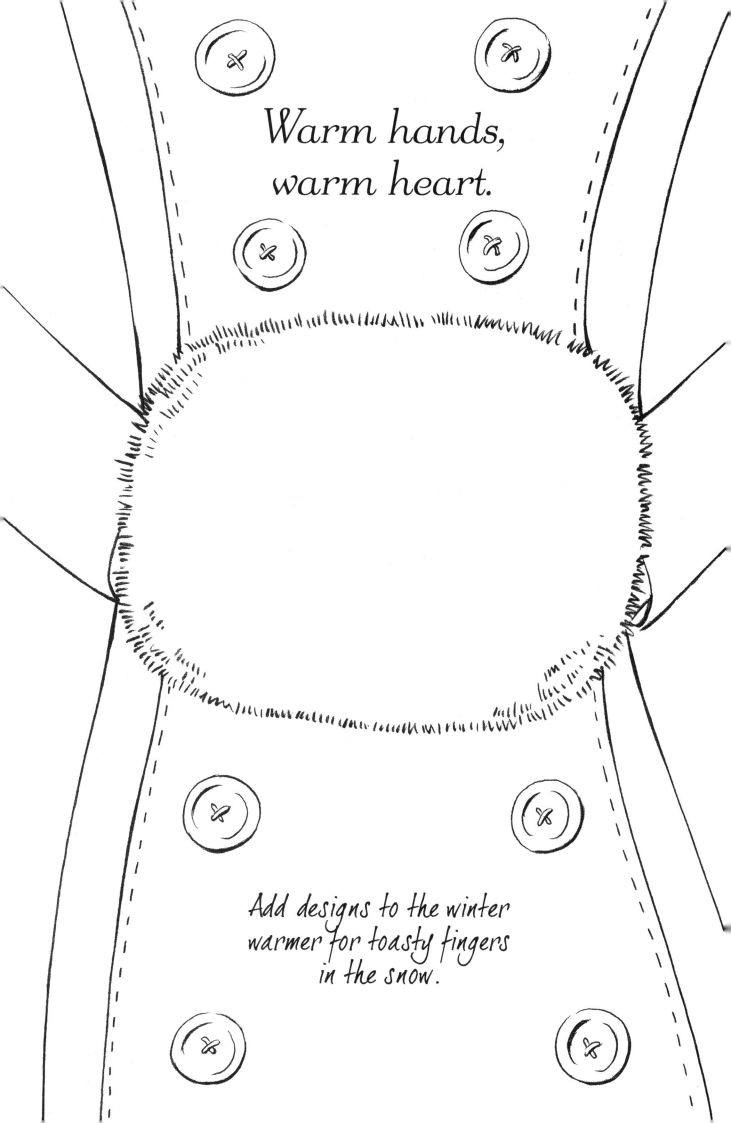

Warm hands,
warm heart.

Add designs to the winter
warmer for toasty fingers
in the snow.

Channel some chalet chic.

Warm up the après-skate look with
a hot chocolate and cool designs.

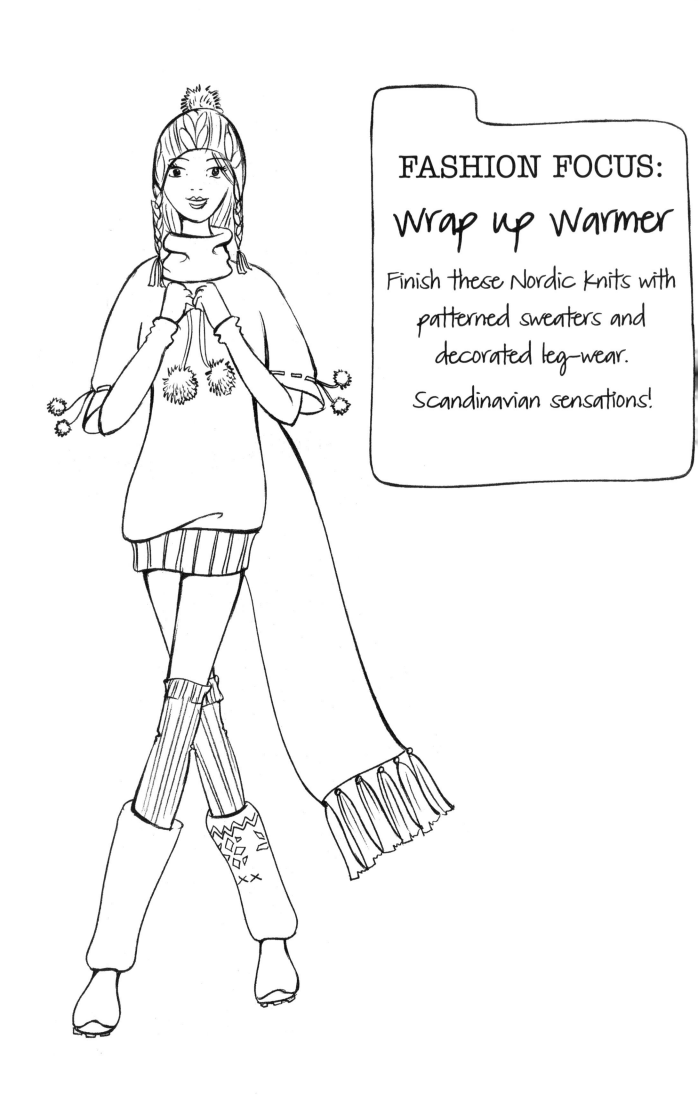

FASHION FOCUS:

Wrap up warmer

Finish these Nordic knits with patterned sweaters and decorated leg-wear.

Scandinavian sensations!

Snow-stoppers!

Make sure these girls
are always chic with
sophisticated ski-wear
for the ultimate in
Alpine elegance and
slalom-style.

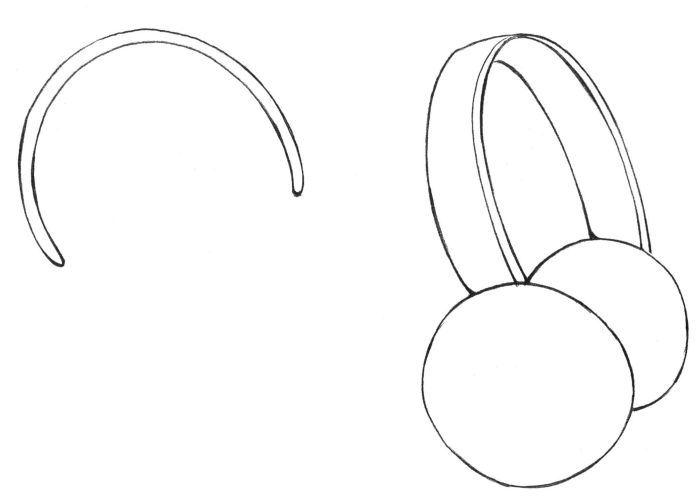

Muffled ears are a must.

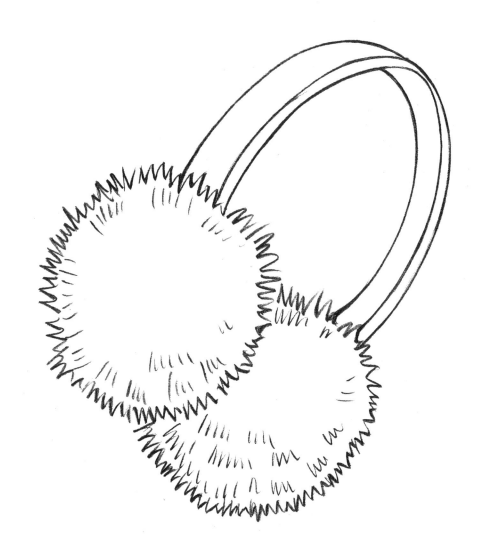

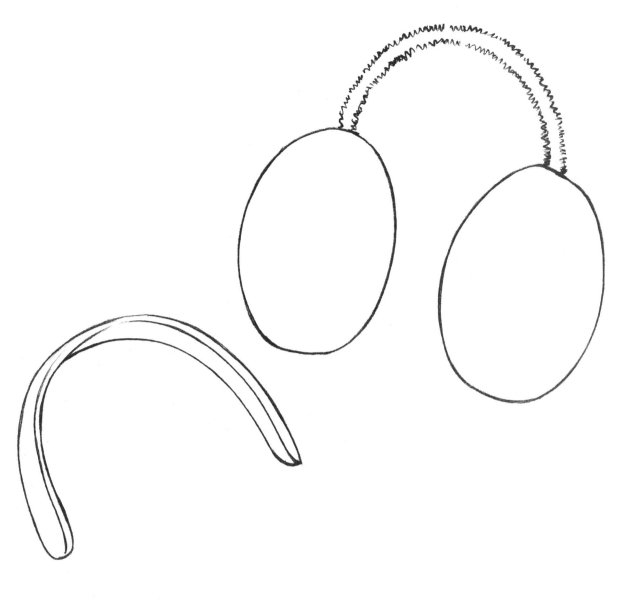

Ears should look fabulous, not frostbitten – add your own designs to make these earmuffs super-stylish.

Create a pattern to give her
coat that extra touch of
winter wonder.

FASHION FOCUS:
Return of the Mac

Complete a classic cut
with your own creative twist
– add patterns and prints
to complete the look.
Terrific trench coats!

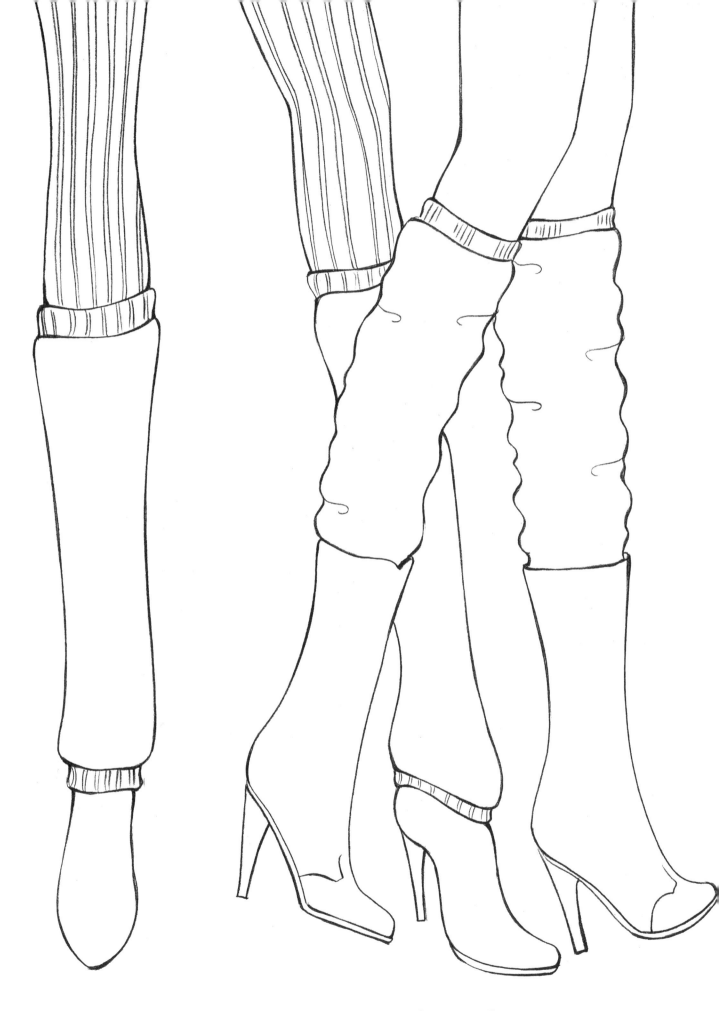

Stepping out in hip hosiery.

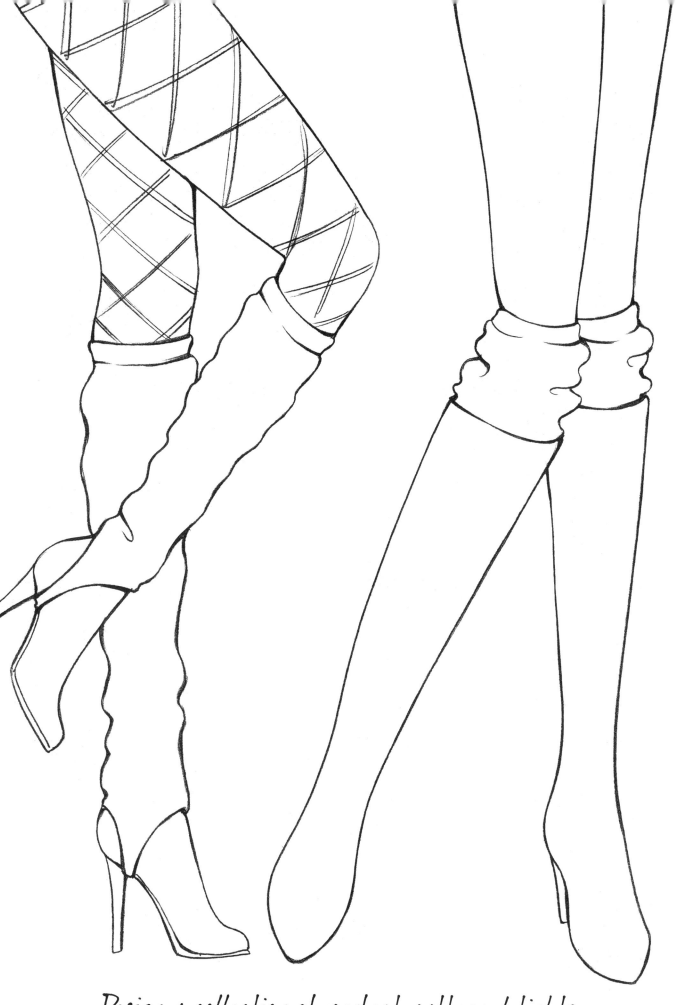

Design a collection of perfect patterned tights
and legwarmers to keep legs warm this winter.

FASHION FOCUS:
So Snow Ball

Add snowflake crystals to make an impact in gowns that shine all night long.

A winter wonderland.

The layered
look for
chilly days.

Snoods and
scarves need
bold patterns
to stand out
from the crowd
- add your
own designs.

THE
RED-CARPET
ISSUE

Best dressed?

Complete their outfits to
make them red-carpet ready.

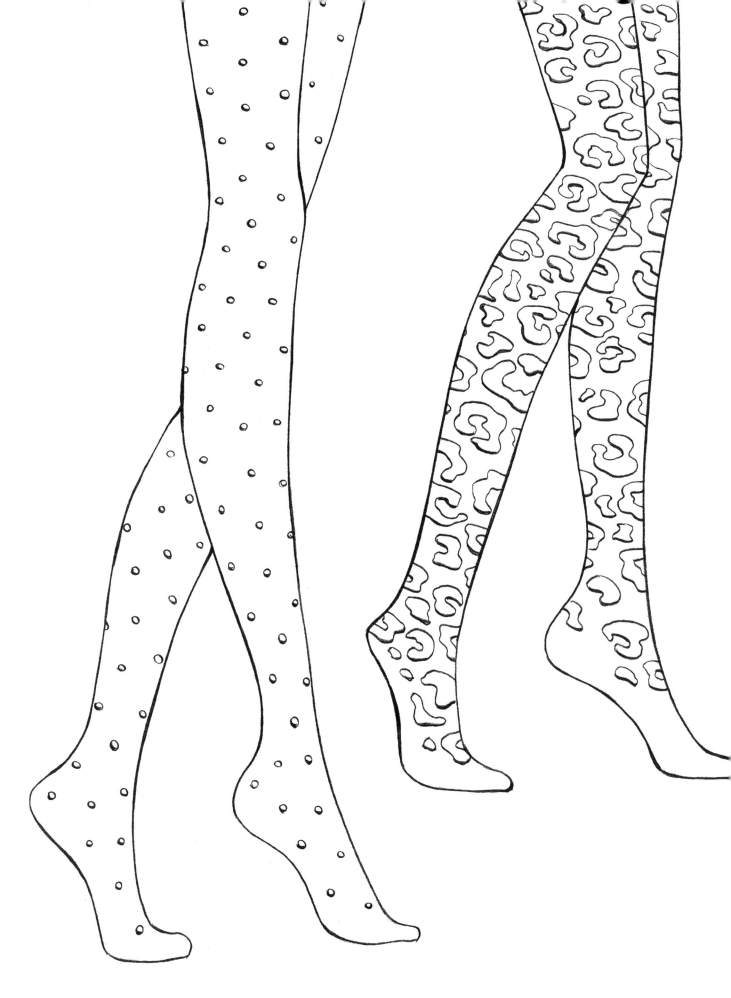

Hot-foot to shoe heaven.

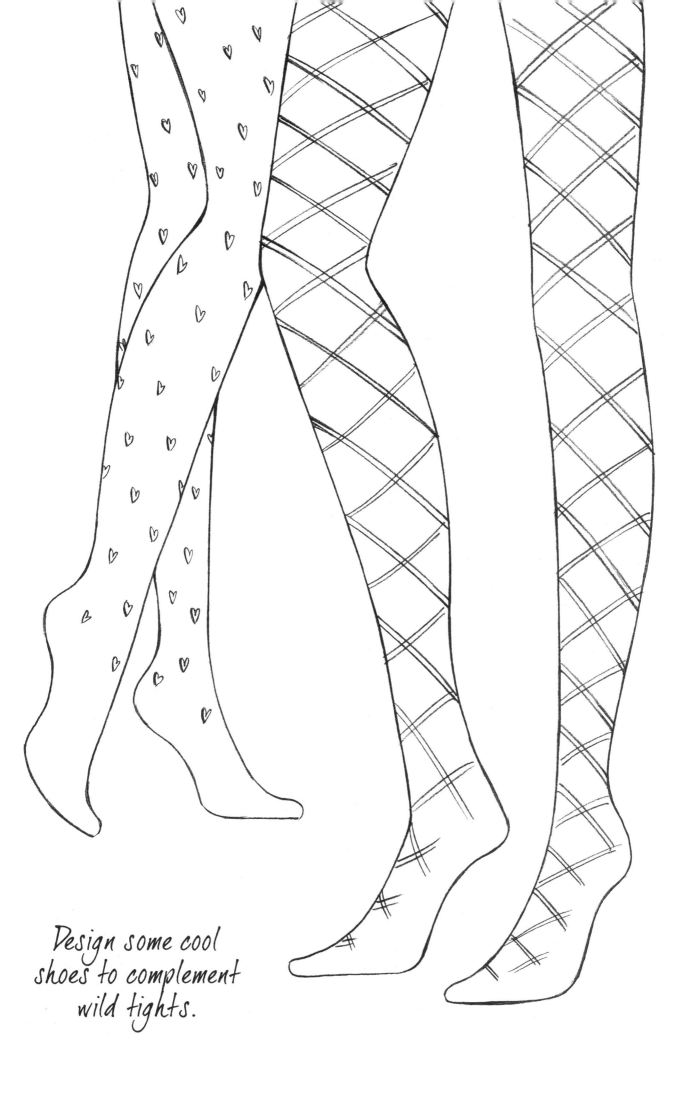

Design some cool
shoes to complement
wild tights.

Design a look tha[t] will steal the sh[ow]

Making an entrance.

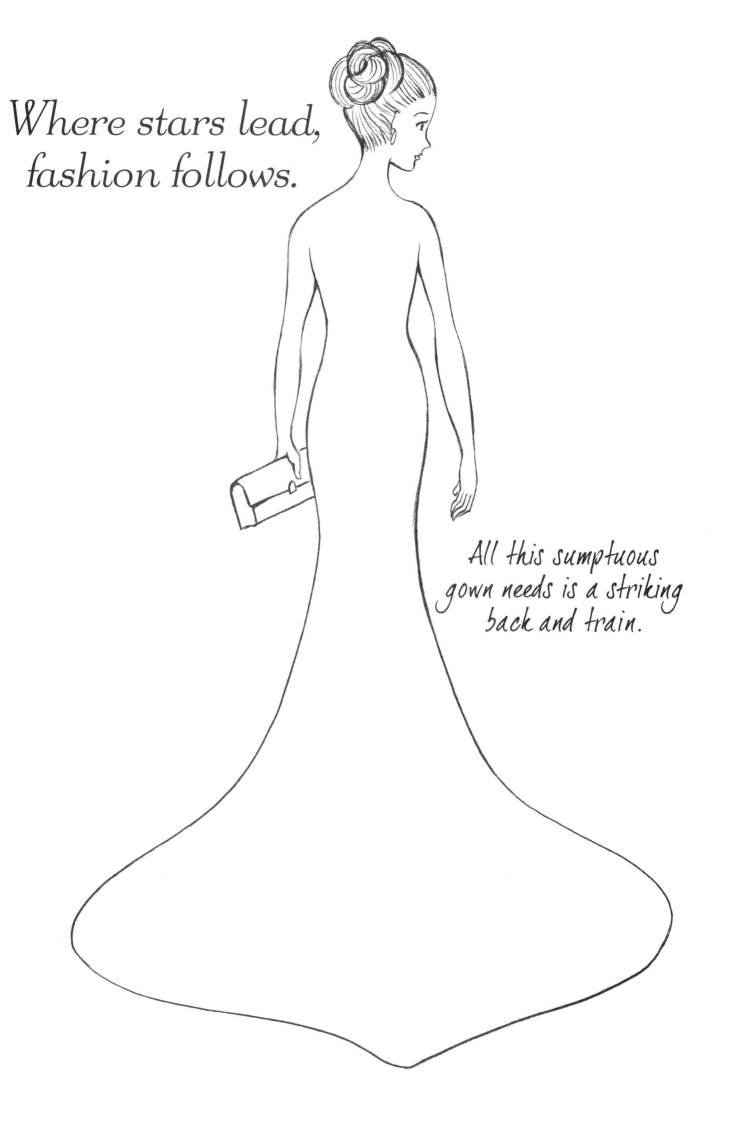

Where stars lead, fashion follows.

All this sumptuous gown needs is a striking back and train.

FASHION FOCUS:
Hollywood Classics

Three fabulous dresses with screen-icon style – bringing the Golden Age of Hollywood up to date.

Premiere-ready.

Only Oscar-worthy
opulence will do.

Complete these dresses
with overlapping folds
of fabric.

Designer draping makes red-carpet
dresses float magically.

FASHION FOCUS:
Dapper Gents

Smart suits and suave
style is the hottest look
for a leading man.

So stunning.

A treasure trove of treats.

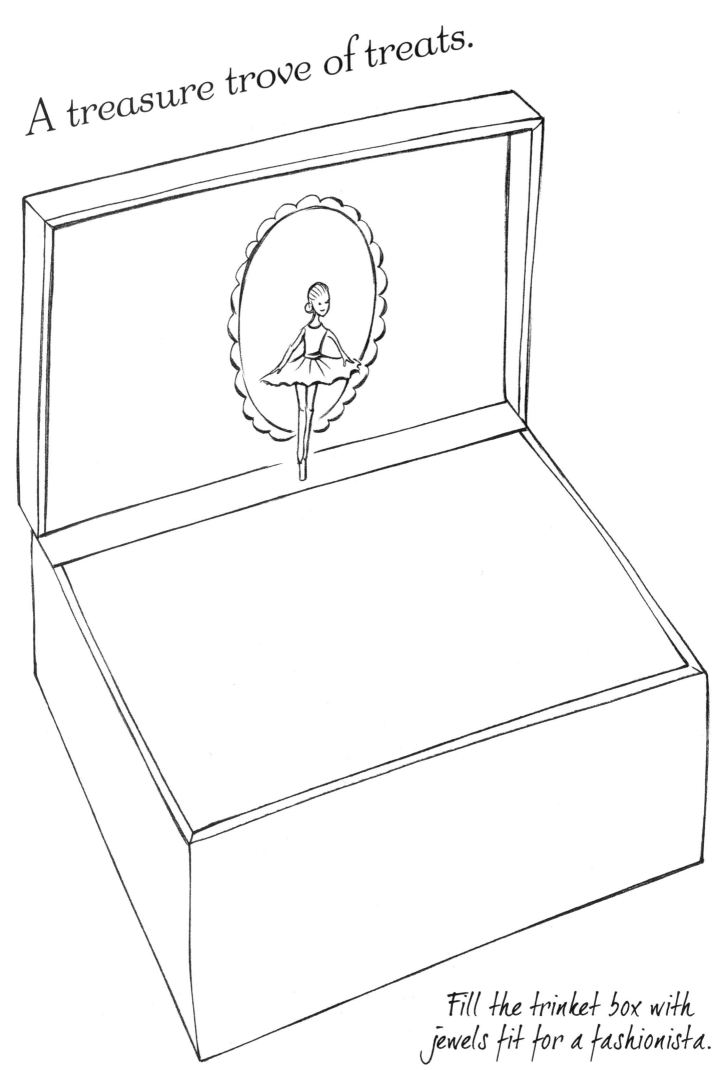

Fill the trinket box with jewels fit for a fashionista.

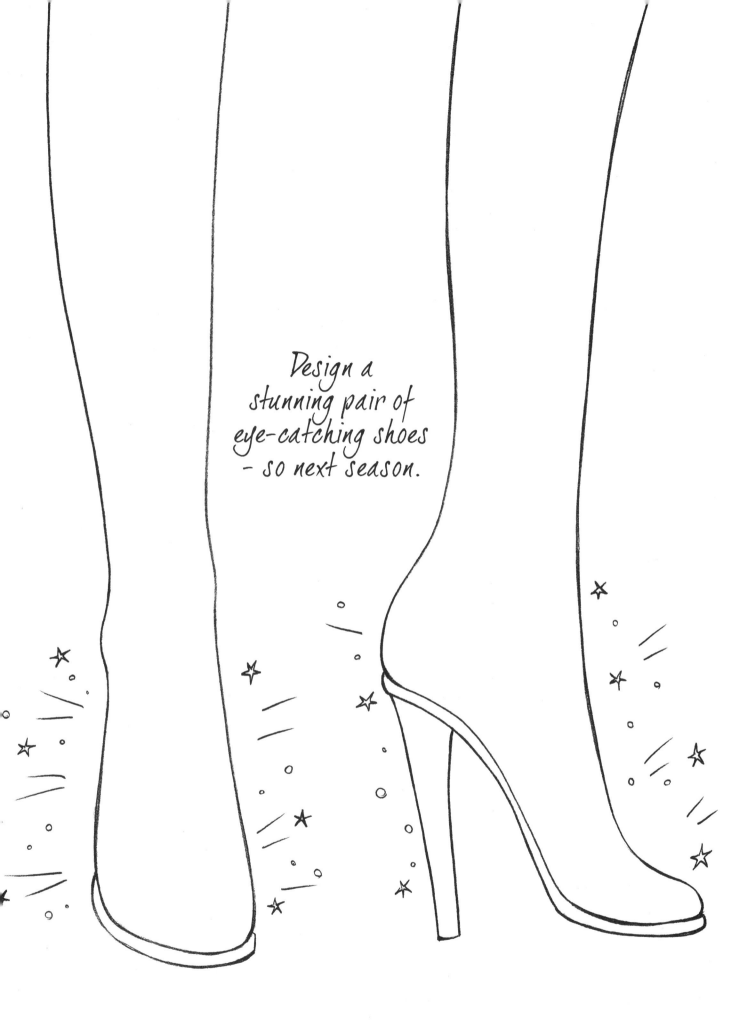

Design a stunning pair of eye-catching shoes – so next season.

Heart these heels.

360 degrees of fascination.

This gown needs a
beautiful back ...

... and a fabulous front.

Bangles of style.

Make these ladies fabulous to the fingertips with beautiful bold bangles and bracelets.

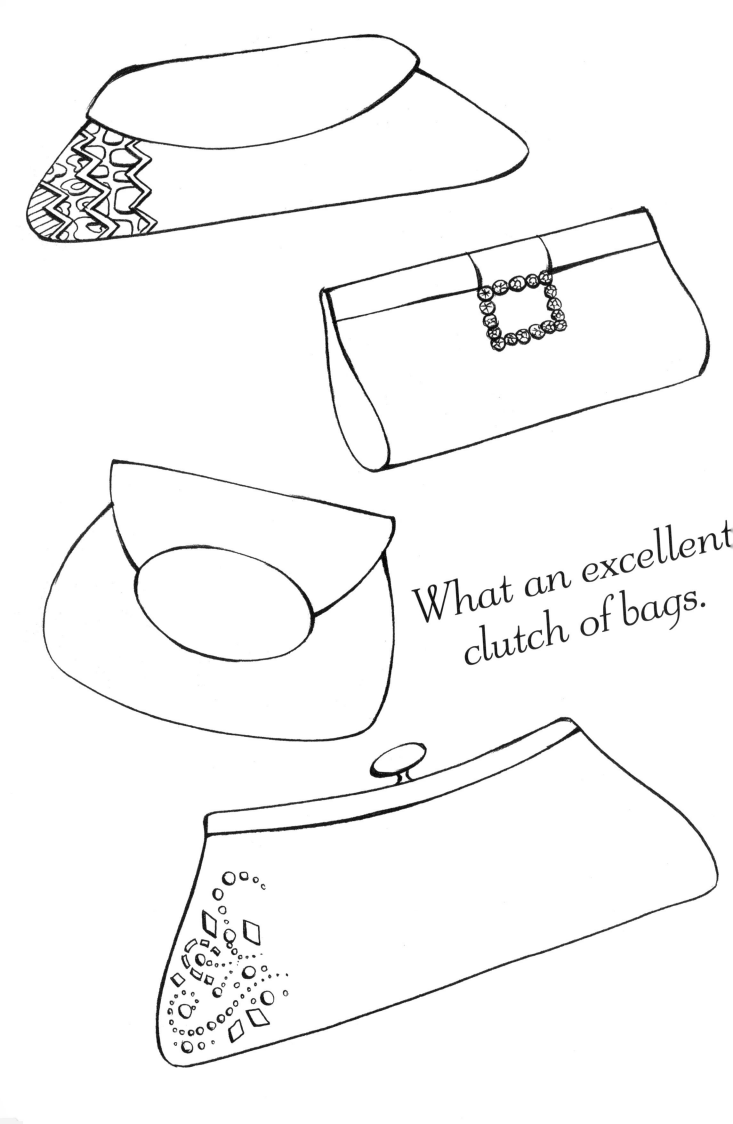

What an excellent clutch of bags.

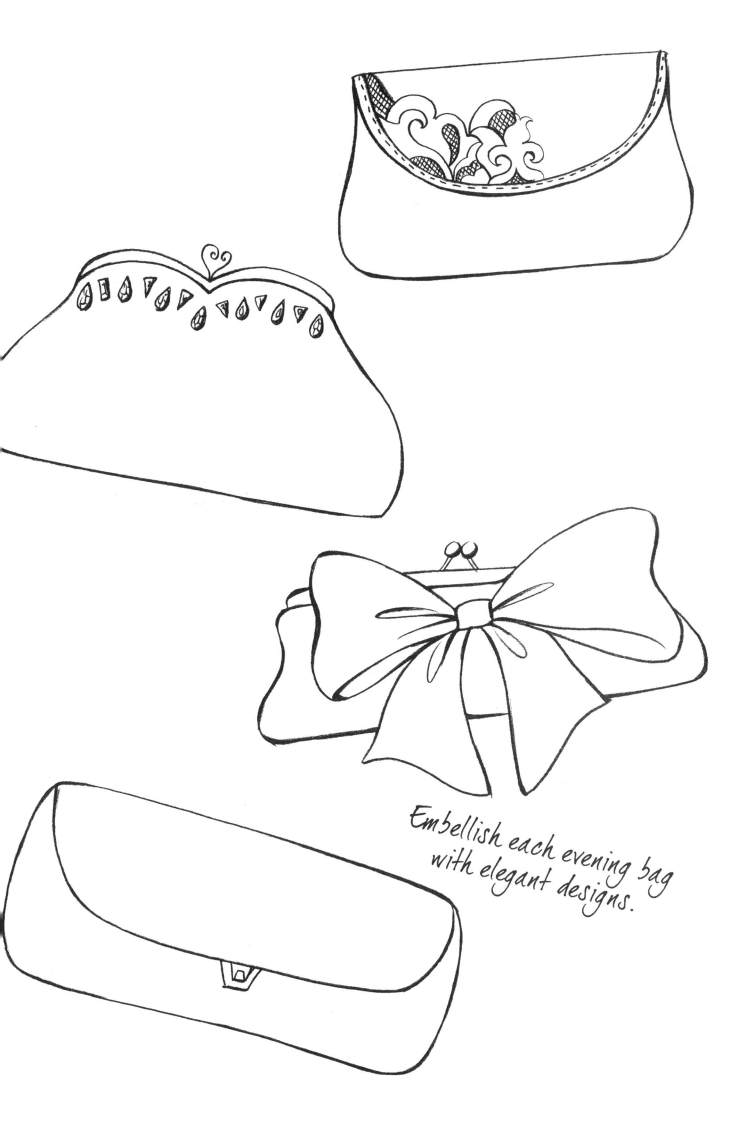

Embellish each evening bag with elegant designs.

Design a
dazzling
necklace
- sure to
turn heads.

Making a statement.